The Cocktail

A comedy

A. R. Gurney

Samuel French - London
New York - Toronto - Hollywood

THE COCKTAIL HOUR

The Cocktail Hour toured Great Britain in 1990 with the
following cast:

Bradley	John McCallum
John	Nicholas Hammond
Ann	Googie Withers
Nina	Joanna McCullum

Directed by **Richard Cottrell**
Designed by **Peter Cooke**

The action of the play takes place during early evening in
autumn in up-state New York

Time—mid seventies

ACT I Bradley and Ann's living room
ACT II The same

For my family

ACT I

The set is basically realistic, but should also be vaguely theatrical, reminding us subliminally of those photographs of American drawing room comedies in the thirties or forties, designed by Donald Oenslager or Oliver Smith. In any case, it is a lovely step-down living room, with an arched entrance leading to a front hall and perhaps the start of a staircase. There is an antique writing desk, a working fireplace with a mantelpiece, a fire bench and a pretty good Impressionist painting hanging over it. The US wall is full of good books, all hard-back, some leatherbound sets, some large art books, all neatly organized. The room also contains a baby grand piano on which are a number of black-and-white family photographs framed in silver or leather: portraits of children, snapshots of children at sports, pictures of dogs, large group shots of families, an occasional faded photograph of a nineteenth century couple. DS, of course, is a large, comfortable couch with a coffee table in front of it, along with several comfortable chairs and a moveable footstool. There might be a corner china cabinet displaying excellent china. All the furniture looks old and waxed and clean. There's a thick, warm, Persian rug on the floor. Through the windows, a few barren branches are seen in the early evening light. The overall effect should not be opulent or grandiose or particularly trendy, but rather tasteful, comfortable and civilized, an oasis of traditional warmth and solid good taste, a haven in a heartless world. On the coffee table, noticeably set apart from the china ashtrays and other objects, is a thick manuscript in a black cover

As the CURTAIN *rises the stage is empty. The light from the windows indicates early evening, early fall*

After a moment Bradley enters, carrying a silver ice bucket. He is in his seventies and very well-dressed. He is followed by his son, John, who is in his early forties and more informally dressed. John carries a silver tray with several liquor bottles and glasses on it

Bradley (*turning on the light in the hall*) This is what's called bringing the mountain to Mohammed.

John Right.

Bradley Otherwise we'd have to trek all the way back to the pantry whenever we needed to return to the well.

John Makes sense to me.

Bradley (*setting down the ice bucket on the table behind the couch*) Of course when we had maids, it was different. You could just push the buzzer, and say bring this, bring that, and they'd bring it.

John (*setting down the tray*) I remember.

Bradley Not that they could mix a drink. They couldn't make a martini to save their skin. But they could make ice, bring water, pass cheese. It was very pleasant.

John Before the war.

Bradley That damn war. Those Germans have a lot to answer for. Well. Let's see ... What are we missing? ... Have we got the lemon for your mother's martini?

John (*taking it out of his pocket*) It's right here, Pop.

Bradley Your mother likes a small twist of lemon in her martini.

John I know.

Bradley And my Cutty Sark scotch.

John Oh yes.

Bradley (*looking at the label*) It's a good scotch. Not a great scotch, but a good one. I always enjoy the picture on the label. The American clipper ships were the fastest in the world. Magnificent vessels. Beautifully built. Made our country great.

John The *Cutty Sark* was English, Pop.

Bradley I know that. I'm speaking generally.

John Actually the clipper ships only lasted a few years.

Bradley Not true.

John Only a few—before steam.

Bradley Not true at all.

John I think so, Pop.

Bradley I wish your brother were here. He'd know. He knows all there is to know about boats.

John (*going to the bookcase*) I'll look it up.

Bradley Never mind. I said, *never mind*. We are not going to waste the evening in pedantic arguments.

John returns from the bookcase

Now look what I did. I brought out a whole bottle of soda water. Automatically. Thinking your brother *would* be here. Won't drink anything else. Never did.

John Smart man.

Bradley I telephoned him yesterday. Tried to get him to come up. "Come on, Jigger," I said. "Join us. John's coming. Your sister will be here. We'll all have cocktails and your mother will provide an excellent dinner. You can play the piano. We'll all gather around the piano and sing. Bring Sylvia, if you want. Bring the children. I'll pay for the whole thing." But no. Wouldn't do it. Jigger's a very positive person, once he's made up his mind.

John It's a tough trip for him, Pop.

Bradley I know that.

John He's working weekends now. They've put him back in sales.

Bradley We all have to sell. One way or another.

John He's looking for another job.

Bradley I know all that. You don't need to tell me that. I'm in touch with him all the time. (*He returns to the bar*) What'll you have by the way?

John Some of that soda water, actually.

Bradley You?

John That's what I'll have.

Bradley You're the one who likes to tuck it away.

John Not tonight.

Bradley And why not, may I ask?

John It makes me say and do things I'm sorry for later.

Bradley That's the fun of it.

John Not for me.

Bradley You're not in difficulty, are you?

John No.

Bradley You're not in one of those organizations that make you give it up?

John I just like to keep a lid on myself, Pop.

Bradley Suit yourself. (*He pours him a glass of soda water*) Soda water it is. What is it Lord Byron tells us? "Let us have wine and women, mirth and laughter; sermons and soda water the day after" . . . Maybe you'll change your mind later on.

John Maybe I will.

Bradley (*now pouring his own scotch and water very carefully*) Of course, nobody drinks much these days. At least not with any relish. Marv Watson down at the club is now completely on the wagon. You sit down beside him at the big table, and what's he drinking? Orange juice. I said, "Am I confused about the time, Marv? Are we having breakfast?" Of course the poor thing can't hear, so it doesn't make any difference. But you go to parties these days and even the young people aren't drinking. I saw young Kathy Bickford at the Shoemaker wedding. Standing on the sidelines, looking very morose indeed. I went up to her and said, "What's that strange concoction you've got in your hand, Kathy?" She said, "Lemon Squirt." I said, "What?" She said, "Sugar-free, non carbonated Lemon Squirt." So I said, "Now, Kathy, you listen to me. You're young and attractive, and you should be drinking champagne. You should be downing a good glass of French champagne, one, two, three, and then you should be out there on that dance floor, kicking up your heels right with every usher in sight. And after you've done that, you should come right back here, and dance with me!" Of course, she walked away. (*He finishes making his drink*) They all walk away these days. I suppose I'm becoming a tiresome old fool.

John Hardly, Pop.

Bradley Yes, well, I can still keep the ball in the air, occasionally. I gave a toast at the Shoemaker's bridal dinner. It went over very well.

John Mother told me.

Bradley Oh yes. I made a few amusing remarks. I complimented the bride. You know Sarah Shoemaker? She's terribly tall. She towers over the groom. So I began by saying she stoops to conquer.

John That's a good one, Pop.

Bradley Yes, they liked that. I can still get on my feet if called upon. They still want me to be the Master of Ceremonies at the annual fund raiser for the art gallery. They still ask me to do that.

John That's great, Pop.

Bradley Of course, we all know what Emerson says, "The music that can deepest reach, and cure all ills, is cordial speech." Doesn't Emerson tell us that?

John I think he does, Pop.

Bradley You're the publisher in the family. You should know.

John (*going to the bookcase again*) Let me look it up.

Bradley It doesn't matter.

John It'll be right here, in *Bartlett's*. (*He takes down a book*)

Bradley No! We are not going to destroy the rhythm of the conversation with a lot of disruptive excursions to the bookcase.

John (*putting the book back*) OK.

Bradley Besides, I know Emerson said it. I'm positive.

John OK, Pop.

Bradley sits in what is obviously his special chair

Bradley (*after a pause*) Well. Your mother tells me you've written a play.

John That's right.

Bradley Another play.

John Right.

Bradley (*indicating the manuscript on the table*) Is that it?

John That's it.

Bradley Do you think this one will get on?

John I think so.

Bradley Some of them don't, you know.

John I know that, Pop.

Bradley I don't mean just yours. Apparently it's a very difficult thing to get them done.

John That's for sure.

Bradley Of course nobody goes to the theatre any more. Ted Moffat just made a trip to New York to see his new grandson. I said, "Did you go to the theatre, Ted? Did you see any new plays?" He said he did not. He said all they do these days in the theatre is stand around and shout obscenities at each other. And then take off their clothes. Ted said he wouldn't be caught dead at the theatre. And Ted was once a big theatre-goer.

John There's some good stuff down there, Pop.

Bradley For you, maybe. Not for me. (*Pause*) We liked that play of yours we saw in Boston.

John Thanks.

Bradley Done at some college, wasn't it?

John Boston University.

Bradley We liked that one. Your mother particularly liked it. She thought it was quite amusing.

John Tell the critics that.

Bradley Oh well, the critics. They're not infallible.

John I'll keep that in mind, Pop. (*Pause*)

Bradley We liked that little play of yours we saw in New York a couple of years ago.

John I thought you *didn't* like it.

Bradley No, we did. Miserable little theatre. Impossible seats. Impossible bathrooms. But the play had charm.

John Thanks, Pop.

Bradley Or at least the actress did. What was her name again?

John Swoosie Kurtz.

Bradley Yes. Swoosie Kurtz. Amusing name. Amusing actress. I hear she's gone on to do very well. Your mother saw her on television.

John She's great.

Bradley Lovely profile. Lovely shoulders. She was very attractive in your play.

John I'll tell her.

Bradley Yes, do. Tell her your father liked her very much. (*Pause. He eyes the manuscript on the coffee table*) And now you've written another one.

John Tried to.

Bradley Looks a little long.

John They'll make me cut it.

Bradley I hope they make you cut it a good deal.

John They probably will.

Bradley Nobody likes long plays.

John I know that, Pop.

Bradley Everyone likes to get it over with promptly, and go home to bed.

John I know.

Bradley Will Swoosie Kurtz be in this one?

John I doubt it.

Bradley I hope you get someone who's just as much fun.

John This play's a little different, Pop.

Bradley Different? How is it different?

John It's not as light as the others.

Bradley Don't tell me you're getting gloomy in your middle years.

John Not gloomy, exactly, Pop.

Bradley Are people going to scream and shout in this one?

John They might raise their voices occasionally.

Bradley Are they going to take off their clothes?

John No, they won't do that, I promise.

Bradley Put Swoosie Kurtz in it. She wouldn't shout. Though I suppose I wouldn't mind if she took off her clothes.

John This one's about us, Pop.

Bradley Us?

John The family.

Bradley Oh really?

John This one cuts pretty close to home.

Bradley Oh well. I understand that. You have to deal with what you know. I do it when I'm toastmaster. I sometimes mention your mother. I refer occasionally to you children. At the Shoemaker's wedding, I told an amusing story about Jigger.

John This one's about you, Pop.

Bradley Me?

John You.

Bradley Just me?

John No, no. Mother's in it, of course. And Nina. And Jigger's referred to a lot. And I put myself in it. But I think it centres around you.

Bradley Me.

John I thought I better tell you that, Pop.

Bradley And it's going on?

John It's supposed to.

Bradley In New York?

John That's the talk.

Bradley When?

John Soon. Supposedly.

Pause

Bradley Do you use our names?

John Of course not, Pop.

Bradley But it's recognizably us.

John By people who know us.

Bradley What about people who *don't* know us?

John They'll sense it's a personal play.

Pause

Bradley I suppose you make cracks.

John Cracks?

Bradley Wisecracks. Smart remarks.

John Not really.

Bradley "Not really." What does that mean, "not really"?

John I just try to show who we are, Pop.

Bradley Oh, I'm sure. I know what you write. I remember that crack you made about your grandmother in one of your plays.

John What crack?

Bradley You know very well what crack. You poked fun at her. You ridiculed her. My dear sweet mother who never hurt a fly. That gracious lady who took you to the Erlanger Theatre every Saturday afternoon. That saint of a woman without whom you wouldn't even know what a play *was*!

John I didn't ridicule her, Pop.

Bradley People laughed. I was there. I heard them laugh at your grandmother. Complete strangers roaring their heads off at my poor dear mother—I can't discuss it.

John Come on, Pop.

Bradley I don't think you've written anything in your life where you haven't sneaked in a lot of smart-guy wisecracks about our family and our way of life.

John Please, Pop . . .

Bradley That story you wrote at boarding school, that show you did at college . . .

John You never came to that show.

Bradley I didn't want to come. I knew, I *knew* what you'd say.

John It was just fun, Pop.

Bradley Oh yes? Well, your idea of fun and my idea of fun are very different. My idea does not include making fools out of your family.

John Oh Jesus.

Bradley And don't swear! It's demeaning to both of us.

John OK, OK. I'm sorry.

Pause

Bradley And you've found producers for this thing?

John Yes.

Bradley They'll lose their shirt.

John Maybe.

Bradley They'll go completely bankrupt.

John Come on, Pop.

Bradley What did that critic say about your last play? What was his remark?

John He said we weren't worth writing about.

Bradley There you are. You see? Nobody cares about our way of life.

John I care, Pop.

Bradley You? You've never cared in your life. You've gone out of your way *not* to care. Where were you for our fortieth anniversary? Where were you for my seventy-fifth birthday?

John You said not to come.

Bradley I didn't want you snickering in the corner, making snide remarks. Oh God, I should have known. I should have known that's why you came up here this weekend. Not to visit your parents in their waning years. Not to touch base with the city that nourished you half your life. Oh no. Nothing like that. Simply to announce that you plan to humiliate us all in front of a lot of strangers in New York City.

John I came home to get your permission, Pop.

Bradley My permission?

John I haven't signed any contract yet.

Bradley Then don't.

John (*after a moment*) All right, I won't.

Bradley How can I give my permission for a thing like that?

John All right, Pop.

Bradley How can I approve of someone fouling his own nest?

John I don't foul——

Bradley How can I possibly seal my own doom?

John Oh, come on, Pop.

Bradley I suppose I have no legal recourse.

John The play's *off*, Pop.

Bradley I mean, you don't need to write plays anyway. You have a perfectly good job in publishing.

John That just keeps me going, Pop.

Bradley It's a fine job. It's a solid, dependable, respectable job.

John It's not what I really want to do.

Bradley Well, do it anyway. Most men in this world spend a lifetime doing what they don't want to do. And they work harder at it than you do.

John Come on, Pop ...

Bradley After I'm dead, after your mother's dead, after everyone you can possibly hurt has long since gone, then you can write your plays. And you can put them on wherever you want—New York, Hollywood, right here in Memorial Auditorium, I don't care. But not now. Please.

John OK.

Bradley I'm tired.

John OK, Pop.

Bradley I'm not well.

John I know, Pop.

Bradley I'm not well at all.

John Case closed, Pop. Really.

Bradley Thank you very much.

Pause. They are awkward alone

Sure you don't want a drink?

John No thanks.

Pause

Bradley Where's your mother? ... Suddenly I thoroughly miss your mother. (*He goes to the doorway; calling off*) Darling, where are you?

Ann (*off*) I'm bringing cheese!

Bradley (*to John*) She's bringing cheese. (*He eyes the manuscript*) Did you tell her about this play?

John Yes.

Bradley Did she read it?

John She said she didn't want to.

Bradley Why not?

John I'm not sure.

Bradley That's the trouble. We never are, with your mother.

Ann enters, carrying a plate of crackers and cheese. She is a lovely woman, richly and fashionably dressed

Ann There.

Both men immediately get to their feet

I think I may have established a modicum of order in the kitchen. (*She waits for John to move his script out of the way, then puts the plate of hors d'oeuvres on the coffee table*) And now I can at least pretend to relax.

Bradley What would you like to drink, darling?

Ann (*crossing to close the curtains*) After almost fifty years of marriage, you know very well what I'd like.

Bradley After almost fifty years of marriage, I know very well always to ask.

Ann Then I'd like a very dry martini, with plenty of ice——

Ann
Bradley } (*together*)—and a small twist of lemon.

Bradley Thy will be done. (*He goes to the bar and mixes the drink carefully for her*)

Ann (*to John, after she has partially pulled the curtains*) Don't ask me when we'll eat. We are flying on a wing and a prayer in the dinner department.

John Who've you got out there, Mother? Mildred? Agnes? Who?

Ann Neither one, Mildred has broken her hip, and Agnes has gone to meet her maker.

John Aw . . .

Ann What I have, out there, is Agnes's cousin's niece, who arrived in a snappy red convertible, and whose name is Cheryl Marie, and who I suspect has never made gravy in her life.

John We should have just made dinner ourselves, Mother.

Ann Oh yes. "Ourselves." I've heard that one before. "Ourselves" . . . "Ourselves" means me. It means that yours truly is slaving away out there while the rest of you are enjoying the cocktail hour in here. No thank you, John. I believe in paying people to do things occasionally, even if the person paid happens to be named Cheryl Marie. (*She sits on the couch*)

Bradley (*handing her a drink*) Here you are, darling.

Ann Thank you, dear. (*To John*) No, I'm sorry. The cocktail hour is sacred, in my humble opinion. Even when your father and I are home alone, we still have it. In the kitchen. While I'm cooking. (*She holds out her hand automatically for a cocktail napkin*)

Bradley (*handing her a stack of cocktail napkins*) That's why we did the kitchen over. So we could have it in there.

Ann I know you children all think you're too busy to have it.

Bradley You're missing something.

Ann I think so, too.

Bradley (*joining Ann on the couch*) We're never too busy for the cocktail hour.

Ann It allows people to unwind.

Bradley It allows people to sit down together at the end of the day . . .

Ann To talk things over . . . Settle things down . . .

Bradley The bishop used to say—remember this, darling?—Bishop Dow used to say when he came here for dinner that the cocktail hour took the place of evening prayers.

Ann Well, I don't know about that.

Bradley No, he did. That's what he said.

Ann Well, all I know is I cherish it. And now I want to know what I've already missed.

John Nothing.

Bradley We had a brief discussion of the contemporary theatre.

John Which terminated rather abruptly.

Ann (*looking from one to the other*) Oh. (*Pause*) Who'll have some brie? Bradley?

Bradley No, thank you.

Ann John?

John (*pulling up a footstool*) Thanks.

Ann I must say I love the theatre.

Bradley Used to love it.

Ann It used to be very much a part of our lives.

Bradley Years ago. Before the Erlanger Theatre was torn down.

Ann All the plays would come here.

Bradley All the good plays.

John I remember ...

Ann Such wonderful plays. With such wonderful plots. They were always about these attractive couples ...

Bradley And the husband would have committed some minor indiscretion.

Ann Normally the wife did, darling.

Bradley No, no. I think it was he ...

Ann She did it more, sweetie. The *wife* was normally the naughty one.

Bradley Well, whoever it was, they were all very attractive about it. And they'd have these attractive leading ladies ...

Ann Gertrude Lawrence, Ina Claire, Katharine Hepburn ...

Bradley They'd all come here ...

John I remember you talking about them ...

Bradley Your mother played tennis with Hepburn at the Tennis Club.

Ann Oh, I think we hit a ball or two ...

Bradley Your mother beat her.

Ann Oh, I don't think I *beat* her, Bradley.

Bradley You beat Katharine Hepburn, my love.

Ann I think we might have played a little doubles, darling.

Bradley You beat Hepburn, six-three, six-four! *That* I remember!

Ann Well, maybe I did.

Bradley And we met the Lunts.

Ann Oh, the Lunts, the Lunts ...

Bradley They were friends of Bill Hart's. So we all met at the Statler for a cocktail. After a matinee.

Ann They were terribly amusing.

John I remember your telling me about the Lunts.

Bradley They could both talk at exactly the same time ...

They do this, of course

Ann Without interrupting each other ...

Bradley It was uncanny ...

Ann They'd say the wittiest things ...

Bradley Simultaneously ...

Ann And you'd understand both ...

Bradley It was absolutely uncanny.

Ann Of course they'd been married so long ...

Bradley Knew each other so well ...

Ann They made you feel very sophisticated.

They both unconsciously cross their legs at the same time

Bradley (*touching her hand*) They made you feel proud to be married.

Ann Absolutely. I totally agree. (*Pause*) I wish you'd write plays like that, John.

Bradley Won't do it. Refuses to. Simply doesn't want to.

Ann But I mean, there's a real *need*. Jane Babcock went to Connecticut last weekend to vist her old roommate from Westover, and they thought they'd go into New York to see a play. Well, they looked in the paper and there was absolutely nothing they wanted to see. Finally, they decided to take a chance on one of those noisy English musicals. But when they called for tickets, the man said he was going to charge them three dollars extra. Just for telephoning. When they were calling long distance anyway. Well, that did it, of course. They went to the movies instead. And apparently the movie was perfectly horrible. People were shooting each other—in the *face*! . . . and using the most repulsive language while they were doing it, and the audience was composed of noisy teenagers who screamed and yelled and rattled candy wrappers all around them. Finally they walked out and drove back to New Canaan, thoroughly disappointed with each other and the world. Jane said they really didn't snap out of it until they had cocktails.

Bradley It's all over. The life we led is completely gone.

Ann Jane said if one of your plays had been on, John, they would have gone to that. And paid the extra three dollars, too.

John (*glancing at Bradley*) My plays are a sore subject, Mother.

Ann Oh dear.

Bradley A very sore subject.

Ann Yes, well, it seems that John at least makes some attempt to write about things we know.

Bradley Oh yes. Undercutting, trivializing . . .

Ann Oh now, darling . . .

Bradley (*looking warily at the manuscript*) What's it called, this play?

John It's called *The Cocktail Hour*, actually.

Bradley It's called the *what*?

John *The Cocktail Hour.*

Bradley That's a terrible title.

Ann Oh now, sweetheart . . .

Bradley Terrible.

John Why is it terrible?

Bradley To begin with, it's been used.

John That's *The Cocktail PARTY*, Pop. That's T. S. Eliot.

Bradley Even worse. We walked out on that one.

Ann This is *The Cocktail HOUR*, darling.

Bradley Doesn't make any difference.

Ann No, it does. A cocktail *party* is a public thing. You *invite* people to a cocktail party. A cocktail *hour* is family. It's private. It's personal. It's very different.

Bradley Nobody will know that. It will confuse everyone. They'll come expecting T. S. Eliot, and they'll get John. Either way, they'll want their money back.

John They won't want anything back, Pop. I'm putting it on the shelf. Remember?

Ann On the shelf?

Bradley Where I hope it will remain for a very long time.

Ann Is that the solution?

Bradley That's the solution. We've agreed on that, that's what we've agreed on.

He goes into the hall to check the barometer

Ann Oh dear. (*Pause*) How's Ellen, by the way?

John Fine.

Ann I wish she had come along.

John She had a conference today, Mother.

Ann Oh, I think that's wonderful. I wish I'd had a job when I was young.

Bradley (*from the hall*) All changing, all going . . .

Ann And how are the children?

John Fine. Getting on. Growing up. Charlie already plans to go all the way out to the University of Colorado.

Bradley All gone . . . Married couples leading totally different lives. Children scattered all over the map . . .

Ann I wish you'd brought them all along.

Bradley returns to the room

Bradley I wish Jigger had come.

Ann I wish everyone had come. John's family, Jigger's . . .

Bradley We could have made this a family reunion.

John Which is another play by T. S. Eliot.

Bradley (*crossing to the piano*) I don't care about that. All I know is that if Jigger had come, we'd be gathered around the piano right now. We'd be singing all the old songs. *Kiss Me, Kate—Southern Pacific* . . .

John It's "*South*" Pacific, Pop.

Bradley Whatever it is, Jigger could play it. I miss him. I miss him terribly.

Ann We miss *all* the family, Bradley. Everyone.

Bradley Yes. That's right. Of course. (*To John, indicating the photographs on the piano*) You have that lovely wife, you have those fine, strapping children, do you ever write about them? Do you ever write about how hard your wife has worked over those children? Do you ever tell how your son pitched a no-hitter in Little League? How your sweet Elsie won the art prize? Do you ever write about your brother winning the Sailing Cup? Do we ever hear anything good in your plays? Oh no. Instead you attack your parents in their old age.

John It's not an *attack*, Pop.

Ann (*quickly*) What if you turned it into a book, John? Books aren't quite so public. Billy Leeming wrote some book about *his* parents, and our local bookstores didn't even bother to carry it. Is it all right if he puts us in a book, Bradley?

John I can't write it as a book.

Ann You can certainly try. (*To Bradley*) It seems a shame to waste all that work.

Bradley (*looking out of a window*) Where's Nina? Where's our daughter? She's normally right on time.

Ann I think she had to do something with Portia. She'll be here. Meanwhile, I'd like another drink, Bradley. A weak one—but nonetheless, another.

John I'll get it.

Ann No, your father likes to get it.

Bradley While I still can. (*He bends over to get her glass with some difficulty*)

John Your back OK, Pop?

Ann He's got a pinched nerve.

Bradley Your mother thinks it's a pinched nerve.

Ann Dr Randall thinks it's a pinched nerve.

Bradley Well, I think it's something far more serious.

John What do you think it is, Pop?

Bradley Never mind. We'll call it a pinched nerve because that makes people more comfortable. We'll settle for a pinched nerve. (*He goes to mix Ann's drink*)

Ann (*silently mouthing the words to John*) It's a pinched nerve.

Bradley (*mixing her drink*) And when I was in the hospital with double pneumonia, it was just a cold. I was lying there half-dead with a temperature of one hundred and four, and people would telephone, very much concerned, and your mother would say, "Oh, he's fine, he's perfectly fine, it's just a cold." When they're lowering me into my grave, she'll tell all my friends that it's hay fever. (*He works on her drink*)

Ann (*eyeing the manuscript*) I suppose I should at least read the thing.

John Don't if you don't want to.

Ann Maybe if I read it, it wouldn't seem so frightening.

Bradley Who's frightened? Nobody's frightened.

Ann Trouble is, it's always so painful, John. Reading your things. And seeing them acted, it's even worse. With all those people *watching*.

Bradley It won't be acted.

Ann But it should be *done*, Bradley.

Bradley Not this one, please.

Ann But he's written it. It's his *career*.

Bradley (*as he stirs Ann's drink*) It's not his career. Publishing is his career. That's what's paid the bills and brought up those children. That, and considerable help from you and me. What we're talking about here is an amusing little hobby which probably costs more than it brings in. Which is fine. We all have hobbies. I like my golf. I like to travel. But I don't use my hobby to attack my parents or make them look foolish in the eyes of the world.

Ann finally gets her drink out of his hands

John It's not a hobby! And I don't attack!

Bradley Well, I don't care. I don't want to be on some stage. I don't want to have some actor imitating me. I've got very little time left on this earth . . .

Ann Oh, Bradley . . .

Bradley Very little. Much less than anyone thinks.

Ann Now stop that, Bradley.

Bradley And I don't want people laughing at me, or critics commenting about me, or the few friends I have left commiserating with me in these final days. I don't want that, John. I'm sorry. No.

He crosses to sit in his chair

Ann One thing, John. If you don't do it, you won't get your name in the paper. And that's a good thing, in my humble opinion. I've never liked the publicity which happens with plays. It always seemed slightly cheap to me.

Bradley Of course it is.

Ann And it's dangerous. People read your name, and think you're rich, and rob you. Peggy Fentriss had her name in the paper for her work with the Philharmonic, and when she went to Bermuda, these burglars backed up a whole truck. They even took a grapefruit she left in the refrigerator.

Bradley (*suddenly*) What do you stand to lose if you don't put this thing on?

John (*ironically*) Just my life, that's all, Pop. Just my life.

Bradley Money. I'm talking about money. How much money would you make on it?

John You can't tell, Pop.

Bradley Give me an educated guess.

John Oh . . . A little. If we're lucky.

Bradley "A little. If we're lucky." What kind of an answer is that? No wonder you never went into business.

John I don't *know*, Pop.

Ann I don't see why we have to talk about money, Bradley.

Bradley What's the average amount of money you've made on your other plays?

John Average?

Bradley Give me an average amount . . . Five thousand? Ten? What?

John Pop . . .

Bradley (*crossing to the desk*) I will give you a cheque for twenty thousand dollars right now for not putting on that play.

Ann Bradley!

Bradley Twenty thousand dollars . . . (*He sits down at the desk, finds his cheque book, makes out a cheque*)

John Oh, Pop . . .

Ann (*putting down her drink*) Twenty *thousand*!

Bradley You can't cash it, of course, till Monday, till I've covered it from savings, but I am hereby giving you a cheque.

John I don't want a cheque.

Bradley Well, you might as well take it, because if you don't, I'll simply leave you twenty thousand extra in my will.

Ann Oh, Bradley, now stop it!

Bradley (*holding out the cheque to John*) Here. It's a good deal. You'll be twenty thousand to the good, and you can still put the thing on after I'm dead.

John (*walking away from it*) Pop, I can't . . .

Bradley (*following him*) And if you invest it, you'll have the interest besides, which you wouldn't have otherwise.

Ann I can't stand this.

John I don't want that money, Pop!

Bradley And I don't want that play! I want some peace and privacy in the few days I have left of my life. And I'm willing to pay for it. Now there it is. (*He puts the cheque on the table by his chair*) If you have any business sense at all, you'll take it. And if you don't want it for yourself, then give it to your children, who I hope will show more respect for you in your old age than you've ever shown for me.

John Oh, Pop, oh, Pop, oh Pop . . .

Nina's voice is heard from the hall

Nina (*off*) Hello!

Ann Ah. There's Nina. (*Calling off*) We're having cocktails, dear! (*To the others*) I think it might be time to change the subject.

Nina enters. She is well-dressed and attractive, in her mid-forties. She removes her raincoat

Nina (*kissing her mother*) I'm terribly sorry I'm late. Portia's in trouble again.

Ann Oh no.

John Who's Portia?

Nina (*kissing her father*) She was up all night, wandering from room to room, sighing and groaning.

Ann Oh no.

Bradley That sweet Portia.

John Who's Portia?

Nina And we also think there's something radically wrong with her rear end. (*She tosses her raincoat on the banister*)

Ann Oh no.

Bradley Poor thing.

John Who the hell is *Portia*?

Nina (*kissing her brother*) Portia is our new golden retriever, and we're very worried about her.

Bradley Portia is a brilliant beast. You should write a play about Portia.

John I could call it *Practical Dogs*. As opposed to *Practical Cats*. By T. S. Eliot.

Bradley What would you like to drink, Pookins?

Nina Just white wine, please.

John I'll get it, Pop.

Bradley (*crossing to the bar*) *I'll* get it. I'm still capable of officiating at my own bar.

Nina Plenty of rocks, please. And plenty of soda water. My stomach is in absolute knots.

John Over Portia?

Bradley Portia is superb. I adore Portia.

Nina Over everything.
Ann Poor Nina, and her nervous stomach.
Nina Let's not talk about my stomach, Mother. Let's talk about John. I hear you've written another play, John. (*She sits on the couch*)
Bradley We're not discussing it.
Nina Why not?
Ann It's a sore subject.
Nina Why?
Ann Apparently it's primarily about you-know-who.
Nina Oh. (*Pause. She sees it on the coffee table*) Is that it?
Ann That's it.

Nina gingerly lifts the cover and looks inside

Nina (*reading*) *The Cocktail Hour*. Hmmm.
Bradley Stupid title.
Nina They'll confuse it with Eliot.
Bradley Exactly, Pookins.
Nina Is it going on?
Bradley No.
Ann Maybe not.
John I came up to ask his permission.
Bradley And I said no.
Nina Hmmm.
Bradley (*bringing her a glass of wine*) Here's your wine, darling.
Nina Thank you. (*Pause*) Is Mother in it?
Ann Apparently I am.
Nina Is Jigger?
Bradley I hope not. (*He sits in his chair*)
John Well, he is. In a way.
Nina Are you in it, John?
John I'm afraid I am.
Bradley I think we've said enough on the subject. I want to know where Ed is, Pookins. I thought Ed would be with you.
Nina Ed's in New York. On business for the bank.
Bradley I see. Well, we'll miss him.
Ann (*now doing her needlepoint*) Oh yes. We'll miss Ed.
Nina (*to John*) Am I in it?
John I think Pop wants us to change the subject.
Bradley Thank you, John.
Nina I just want to know if I'm *in* it.
John Yes, you are.
Nina Oh God.
Bradley Tell us about the children, Pookins. I want to hear about my grandchildren.
Nina They're all fine, Pop. (*She picks up the script and holds it to her ear*)
Ann What are you doing, dear?
Nina I think I heard this thing ticking.
Ann (*laughing*) That's funny.

Nina Do you think we should drop it in a big bucket of water?
Bradley I think we should change the subject. Tell me about Andy. Does he
like his job?
Nina He likes it fine, Pop. (*To John, as she thumbs through the script*) I hate
to think what you do to me in this thing.
John You come out all right.
Nina I'll bet. Am I the wicked older sister?
John No.
Nina Am I the uptight, frustrated, bossy bitch?
John No, no.
Nina Well, what am I, then?
John Actually, you play a relatively minor role.
Ann Sounds like you're lucky, dear.
Bradley Tell me about Wendy. Is Wendy doing well at Williams? Does she
still want to be in business?
Nina Do I get a *name*, at least? What's my name here?
John I call you Diana.
Ann Diana?
John (*to Nina*) Isn't that what you used to wish your name was? The
Goddess Diana, Protectress of Wild Animals.
Ann I knew a Diana Finch once. She used to climb down drainpipes and
hang around drugstores. No, I don't like the name.
Nina Well, it's better than *Nina*, Mother. Which means little Ann. Little
you. Sweet little carbon copy.
Bradley I asked you a question about Wendy, Pookins.
Nina (*impatiently*) She's fine, Pop. (*She continues to thumb*) I only see about
ten pages of Diana here. (*More thumbing*) And in the second act, less than
that.
John It's what's known as a supporting role.
Nina Supporting? What do I support?
Ann I imagine all of us, dear. You give us all support. Which is true.
Bradley May we talk about something else?
Nina Do I get to bring in trays? Or do I just carry a spear?
John You come and go.
Nina Come and go? Mostly go, I'd say, thank you very much. (*She reads*)
"Diana exits huffily." Oh boy, there it is. "Huffily." Jesus, John. (*She gets
up huffily*)
Bradley All right, then. (*He goes to the bookcase, gets a large volume—
"Life's Picture History of World War II"—and takes it to a chair in the
front hall where he begins to thumb through it determinedly*) While all of
you continue to concentrate on one very tiresome subject, I will try to
exercise my mind. Let me know, please, if, as, and when you're willing to
broaden the discussion. (*He turns his back on the group*)
Nina I just think it's interesting I always play a minor role in this family.
Ann That's not true, darling.
John You were the one who always owned the dogs.
Ann We gave you that lovely coming-out party.
John You got that trip to Europe.

Ann You had the most beautiful wedding ...

Bradley (*from the hall*) You got my mother's tea set after she died, Pookins.

John Jigger and I used to call you the Gravy Train Girl.

Nina Well, not any more, apparently.

Ann Maybe you're lucky to get off the hook, dear.

Nina Oh boy, John. I swear. It's the old story. Once again, you and Jigger, who never show up here, who come up once a year for a day or two, *if* we're lucky, when we have to drop everything we're doing and rush to be at your beck and call—once again, you two end up getting all the attention, whereas I, I, who have remained here since I was married, who have lived here all my *life* ... who see Mother and Pop at least once a week, who have them for Christmas and Thanksgiving and even *Easter*, for God's sake ... I, who got Pop to go to a younger doctor ... I, me, who drove Mother all over town for *weeks* after her cataract operation ... Who found them a new cleaning woman when their old one just walked *out*! ... Once again I am told I play a goddamn minor *role*!

Ann Now, now ... Now, now.

Bradley (*from the hall*) You've been a wonderful daughter, Pookins.

Nina (*crossing to the bar*) Wonderful or not, I need another drink.

Ann Be careful, darling. Your stomach.

Nina Oh what difference does that make? Who cares? I just play a minor role. If I get ulcers, they're minor ulcers. If I die, it's a minor death.

John Nina, hey, lookit. I kept trying to build up your part.

Nina I'll bet.

John I did. But I never got anywhere.

Nina Why not?

John I never could get your number.

Bradley (*from the hall*) I don't know why anybody has to get anybody else's number.

John No, I mean, you always seem so content around here.

Nina Con*tent*?

John Good husband. Good kids. Good life. You always came out seeming so comfortable and at home.

Bradley (*from the hall*) I should damn well hope so.

Nina *Me*? Is this *me* you're talking about? Comfortable and at home?

Ann He's giving you a compliment, dear.

Nina Is he? Is that a compliment? Comfortable and at home? Oh boy, that's a laugh. That's a good one, John. Boy, you've really painted me into a corner. Ask Dr Randall how comfortable I am. Ask him to show you the X-rays of my insides. He'll show you what it's like to be at home.

Bradley comes back into the room

Bradley Pookins, sweetheart ...

Nina (*revving up*) Do you know anything about my *life*, John? Have you ever bothered to inquire what I *do* around here, all these years you've been away? Did you know that I am Vice-President of the S.P.C.A.?

Ann *And* on the hospital board. *And* the School for the Blind. *And* the gift shop at the gallery ...

Nina Did you know that I am interested in seeing-eye *dogs*, John? Did you know that? I am profoundly interested in them. I'm good with dogs, I'm the best, everyone says that, and what I want to do more than anything else in the world is go to this two-year school in Cleveland where you do nothing but work with seeing-eye dogs.

Ann You can't just commute to Cleveland, darling.

Nina I *know* that, Mother.

John Why can't you?

Nina Because I have a husband, John. Because I have a—*life*!

Bradley And a very good life it is, Pookins.

Nina I mean, what am I supposed to *do*, John? Start subsidizing Eastern Airlines every other *day*? Live in some *motel*? Rattle around some strange city where I don't know a *soul*? Just because I want to work with . . . because I happen to feel an attachment to . . . oh God. (*She starts to cry*)

Bradley (*going to her*) Oh now, Pookins . . . Now stop, sweetie pie . . .

Ann I didn't realize people could get quite so upset about dogs.

Bradley It's not dogs, it's John. (*He wheels on John*) You see what happens? You arrive here and within half-an-hour, you've thrown the whole family into disarray. It's happened all your life. Par for the course, my friend. Par for the course. (*He comforts Nina*) Now calm down, sweetheart. He's not going to do the play anyway.

Nina (*breaking away*) Well, he should! He should do one about *me*! You've never written about me, John. Ever. Why don't you, some time? Why don't you write about a woman who went to the right schools, and married the right man, and lived on the right street all the days of her life, and ended up feeling perfectly terrible!

Nina runs out of the room and upstairs

Bradley There you are, John. You satisfied? Will you put that in your play? Or do you still want to concentrate all your guns on your dying father? (*He goes out after Nina; calling*) Wait. Nina. Pookins. Sweetheart . . .

Bradley follows Nina off and upstairs. Pause

Ann (*holding out her glass*) I might have just a splash more, John.

John (*taking her glass*) OK, Mother.

Ann Just a splash. I'm serious.

John (*mixing it*) Right.

Ann You're not having anything?

John Can't seem to get away with it these days, Mother.

Ann What does that mean?

John Very quickly, I turn into an angry drunk.

Ann Good heavens. Why is that?

John I don't know . . . (*He looks where his father has gone*) I guess I'm sore about something. (*Pause*) Is he as sick as he says he is, Mother?

Ann You know your father.

John He keeps saying he's dying.

Ann He's been saying that for years. He announced it on his fortieth birthday. He reminds us of it whenever he gets a cold. Lately, when we go to bed, he doesn't say "goodnight" any more. He says, "goodbye," because he thinks he won't last till morning.

John But you think he's OK?

Ann I think ... No, I *know*, we all know, that he has a blood problem, a kind of leukemia, which seems to be in remission now. Somehow I don't think that will kill him. Something else will.

John You think my play will?

Ann *He* seems to think it will.

John Oh God ...

Ann And *you* must think it might, John. Otherwise you never would have bothered to clear it with him.

John I almost wish I hadn't.

Ann I'm glad you did. It shows you have strong family feelings.

John Family feelings, family feelings! The story of my life! The bane of my existence! Family feelings. Dear Mother, dear Pop. May I have permission to cross the street? May I have permission to buy a car? Would you mind very much if I screwed my girl?

Ann Now that's enough of that, please.

John Well, it's true! Family feelings. May I have your approval to put on a play? Oh God, why did I come here? Why did I bother? Most playwrights dish out the most brutal diatribes against their parents, who sit proudly in the front row and applaud every insult that comes along. Me? Finally— after fifteen years of beating around the bush—I come up with something which is—all right, maybe a little on the nose, maybe a little frank, maybe a little satiric at times—but still clearly infused with warmth, respect, and an abiding affection, and what happens? I'm being censored, banned, bribed not to produce.

Ann I still wish you'd make it a book.

John Oh, Mother ...

Ann No, I'm serious. Books are quieter.

John I can't write books.

Ann You work on them all the time.

John But I can't write them.

Ann Plays are so noisy.

John I know.

Ann They cause such attention.

John I know.

Ann I didn't mean just for us. I mean for you, as well.

John I know, Mother.

Ann Those reviews must hurt terribly. The bad ones.

John They do.

Ann All coming out together. Wave after wave. Every little suburban newspaper putting in its two-cents worth. And they can all be so mean.

John Right.

Ann Book reviewers seem kinder, somehow. You have the feeling that people who write books get their friends to review them.

John Yes ...

Ann But not with plays. I mean, who *are* those people who review plays? What do they do when they're not sitting around criticizing?

John I hear some of them are decent folks, Mother.

Ann They well may be, but I don't think they have the faintest notion what you're writing about.

John Sometimes they don't seem to.

Ann They don't like us, John. They resent us. They think we're all Republicans, and all superficial, and all alcoholics.

John I know.

Ann (*taking a sip; with a twinkle*) Only the latter is true.

John laughs, possibly hugs her

I also think . . .

John What?

Ann Never mind.

John No, come on, Mother. What?

Ann I also think he's scared you'll spill the beans.

John The beans?

Ann The beans.

John What beans?

Ann Oh, John, face it. Everyone's got beans to spill. And, knowing you, you'll find a way to spill ours.

John I'm simply trying to tell the truth, Mother.

Ann Fine. Good. But tell the truth in a *book*. Books take their time. Books *explain* things. If you have to do this, do it quietly and carefully in a book.

John I can't, Mother.

Ann You can try.

John I *can't*. Maybe I'm a masochist, but I can't seem to write anything but plays. I can't write movies or television. I'm caught, I'm trapped in this old medium. It's artificial, it's archaic, it's restrictive beyond belief. It doesn't seem to have anything to do with contemporary American life. I feel like some medieval stone cutter, hacking away in the dark corner of an abandoned monastry, while everyone else is outside, having fun in the Renaissance. And when I finish, a few brooding inquisitors shuffle gloomily in, take a quick look, and say, "That's not it. That's not what we want at all!" Oh, God, why do I do it? Why write plays? Why are they the one thing in the world I want to do? Why have I always done them?

Ann Not always, John. You used to write the most marvellous letters, for example. From camp. From boarding school . . .

John But I wrote plays long before that. Long before I could even write, I put on plays.

Ann Oh well. Those things you did down in the playroom.

John They were *plays*, Mother. I'd clear the electric trains off the ping-pong table so it could be a stage. And I'd use up all the crayons in the house doing the scenery. And use up all my allowance bribing Nina and Jigger to be in them.

Ann And then you'd drag your father and me down and we'd have to sit through the damn things.

John But they were plays, Mother.

Ann Yes. I suppose they were.

John What were they about, Mother? Do you remember?

Ann I do not.

John My psychiatrist keeps asking me what they were about. He says they could open a few doors for me, but I've blocked them all.

Ann I wish you'd block that psychiatrist.

John But if there was a pattern to the plots, if there was some common theme to what I was doing, it would . . .

Ann It would what?

John Explain things . . . I wish you could remember. (*Pause*)

Ann You always gave yourself a leading part, I remember that.

John I'll bet.

Ann And it seems to me you always played this foundling, this outsider, this adopted child . . .

John Is that true?

Ann I think so. Your father and I would roll our eyes and think, what have we wrought. I mean, on you'd come, this poor prince who'd been adopted by beggars. Or else . . .

John What?

Ann I remember one particularly silly one. You were the court jester. You put on a bathing suit and a red bathing cap and started dancing around, being very fresh.

John Hold it. Say that again. What did I wear?

Ann You wore your little wool bathing trunks from *Best and Company*, and Nina's red bathing cap.

John *The Red-Headed Dummy*.

Ann I suppose.

John No, I mean that was the title of my play: *The Red-Headed Dummy*! It's coming back!

Ann Well, whatever it was, I remember it went on for*ever*! It made us late for dinner somewhere.

John Good God, Mother, I suddenly realize what I was doing in that play.

Ann Well, *I* certainly don't.

John I think I know! And I think my shrink would agree!

Ann I'm all ears.

John It's a little Freudian, Mother. It's a little raw.

Ann Then I'm not terribly interested. (*Pause*) What?

John What I was doing was parading my penis in front of my parents.

Ann Oh, John, honestly.

John I was! The bathing suit, the red cap, *The Red-Headed Dummy*! Get it? I was doing a phallic dance.

Ann John, don't be unattractive.

John No, no, really. I was playing my own penis. Smart kid, come to think of it. How many guys in the world get a chance to do that? Especially in front of their parents.

Ann I think it's time to turn to another topic.

John No, but wait. Listen, Mother. I'll put it in a historical context. What I was doing was acting out a basic, primitive impulse which goes back to the Greeks. That's how comedy *originated*, Mother! The phallic dance! These peasants would do these gross dances in front of their overlords to see what they could get away with! And that's what I was doing, too, at three-years-old! Me! The Red-Headed Dummy! Dancing under the noses of my parents, before they went out to dinner! Saying, "Hey, you guys. Look. Look over here. I'm here, I'm alive, I'm wild, I have this penis with a mind of its own!" That's what I was doing then! That's what I've always done! That's what I'm doing right now, right in this room! And that's why I have to write plays, Mother. I have to keep doing it.

Long pause

Ann Are you finished, John?

John For now, at least.

Ann All right, then, I want to say this: I don't like all this psychological talk, John. I never have. I think it's cheap and self-indulgent. I've never liked the fact that you've consulted a psychiatrist, and your father agrees with me. It upsets us very much to think that the money we give you at Christmas goes for paying that person rather than for taking your children to Aspen or somewhere. I don't like psychiatrists in general. Celia Underwood went to one, and now she bursts into tears whenever she plays bridge. Psychiatrists make you think about yourself too much. And about the bedroom too much. There's no need!

John Mother——

Ann No, please let me finish. Now I want you to write, John. I think sometimes you write quite well, and I think it's a healthy enterprise. But I think you should write *books*. In books, you can talk the way you've just talked and it's not embarrassing. In books, you can go into people's minds ... Now we all have things in our lives which we've done, or haven't done, which a book could make clear. I mean, I myself could tell you ... I could tell you ... I could tell you lots of things if I knew you would write them down quietly and carefully and sympathetically in a good, long book ...

Bradley enters

Bradley What book?

Ann We were just talking about the value of a good book, dear.

Bradley (*crossing to his chair*) I agree with you. I'm reading the Bible now, John. I keep it right by my bed. It's surprisingly good reading. And excellent insurance.

Ann How's Nina? And where's Nina?

Bradley Nina is fine. Nina is dealing with a slight confusion in the kitchen.

Ann (*jumping up*) I knew it. I could feel it in my bones. Tell me what happened.

Bradley There was a slight misunderstanding about the oven.

Ann Explain that, please.

Bradley The oven was inadvertently turned off.

Ann You mean that beautiful roast of beef . . .

Bradley Is at the moment somewhat underdone.

Ann Oh, I could cry.

Bradley Now don't *worry*, darling. The oven is now working overtime. And there's even talk of Yorkshire pudding.

Ann How can that creature make Yorkshire pudding if she can't cook a simple roast?

Bradley Because I asked her to, darling. And because I presented her with another package of peas from the deep freeze.

Ann Why more peas? What happened to the peas she had?

Bradley I'm afraid there was a lack of attention to the right rear burner, darling.

Ann Oh, I can't *stand* this! We'll be lucky if we eat by nine! I should have known never to take a chance on someone named Cheryl Marie!

She hurries out, adlibbing about the roast beef

Bradley (*calling after her*) Her name is Sharon, dear. *Sharon* Marie. (*Pause; to John*) Do you have any servants in this play of yours?

John Not really.

Bradley "Not really?" What does that mean, "Not really?" Does your producer have to pay for a maid or not?

John No, he doesn't, Pop.

Bradley Probably just as well. Knowing you, you'd get them all wrong anyway.

John Thanks.

Bradley Well I mean, nobody understands how to treat servants today. Even your mother. She was born with them, they brought her breakfast in bed until she married me, and I'm afraid she takes them too much for granted. Your generation is worse. You don't even seem to know they're there. Now I went out just now and spoke personally to Sharon Marie. I inquired about her life. And because I took the time to converse with her, because I made her feel part of the family, you may be sure we will have a much more delicious dinner.

John And because you tipped her twenty bucks.

Bradley Yes. All right. I did that, too. Because I firmly believe good service is important. You can't live without servants. At least you can't live well. Civilization depends on them. They are the mainstay of intelligent life. Without them, you and I would be out in the kitchen right now, slicing onions and shouting over the Dispose-All, and none of this would be taking place at all.

John You're probably right.

Bradley Of course I'm right. (*Pause*) I did something else while I was out there, besides buttering up Sharon Marie.

John What else did you do?

Bradley I put in a call to your brother.

John Ah.

Bradley Couldn't get him, of course. He's still with a client. Seven-thirty on a Saturday night. Yes, well, we all have to work. We all have to put our shoulder to the wheel. No substitute for good hard work. When the head of General Motors dies, they hire a new office boy.

John You think that's true, Pop?

Bradley Of course it's true. Or was, until your friend Roosevelt came along and gave everyone a free ride.

John Hey, now wait a minute . . .

Bradley I can't discuss it. Anyway, I spoke to Sylvia. She expects Jigger home any minute, and then he'll call.

John Good.

Bradley So when he calls, we can all talk to Jigger. If we can't gather around a piano, we can still gather around a telephone.

John Fine.

Bradley goes to the bar to make himself another drink

Bradley I wish you'd have a drink.

John No thanks, Pop.

Bradley It will still be quite a while before we eat.

John I can last.

Bradley (*as he makes his drink*) I hate to drink alone.

John That's OK.

Bradley As you know, I have very firm rules about alcohol. Never drink before six. Never drink after dinner. And never drink alone. You make me feel like an old souse.

John I'll have wine, then, Pop.

Bradley Good. It's a convivial thing, drinking together. Even if it's just white wine.

John Have you got any red there, Pop?

Bradley Red?

John I don't like white that much.

Bradley You mean I have to go all the way out and open a whole new bottle of red wine?

John OK, Pop. A drop of scotch, then.

Bradley (*pouring a glass*) A little scotch. (*He pours a strong one*)

John A *little*, Pop? That looks like a double.

Bradley You can't fly on one wing.

John Fly? Should I fasten my seat-belt?

Bradley Maybe I just want to have a good, healthy belt with my older son before the evening's over.

John OK. (*He raises his glass to his father, takes a sip. It is obviously strong*) Ah.

Bradley (*looking at the cheque*) I notice my cheque is still there.

John I don't want it, Pop.

Bradley Take it. I insist.

John I don't want it. (*Pause*)

Bradley (*settling into his chair*) Tell me a little more about your play.

John (*on the couch*) It's not going on. I promise.

Bradley I just want to know a little more about it.

John Pop, we'll just get into trouble . . .

Bradley No, no, we're mature individuals. We're having a drink together at the end of the day ... For example, does it have a plot?

John Not much of one, actually.

Bradley I like a good plot.

John I can't seem to write them.

Bradley I remember learning at Yale: there are three great plots in Western literature: *Oedipus Rex*, *Tom Jones* and I forget the third.

John Ben Johnson's *Volpone*.

Bradley No, it wasn't that.

John According to Coleridge, those are the three great plots.

Bradley No, no.

John I've just *edited* a textbook on Coleridge, Pop.

Bradley Well, you're still wrong.

John (*starting to get up*) I could look it——

Bradley No!

John OK.

Pause. They drink

Bradley So you don't have a plot.

John Not much of one.

Bradley You don't try to drag in that business about our family having Indian blood, do you?

John *Do* we?

Bradley We do not. (*Pause*) Though some people keep saying we do.

John What people?

Bradley Your cousin Wilbur, particularly. He used to bandy it about. But it's an absolute lie. There is no Indian blood in our branch of the family. I want that absolutely understood before I die.

John OK.

Bradley Your Great-uncle Ralph may have had a relationship with an Indian woman, but that was it.

John Did he?

Bradley *May* have. Besides, she was an Indian princess. She was very well-born. According to your grandmother, she was quite beautiful. And she sewed very well.

John Sowed corn?

Bradley Sewed moccasins. I don't know what she sewed. The point is that Indian blood never came down through our line. Harry Blackburn down at the club constantly brings it up. He says it accounts for our affinity for alcohol. It's not funny, and I told him so, and if he mentions it again, I'm going to punch him in the nose.

John Take it easy, Pop.

Bradley Anyway, if you bring up that Indian blood stuff in your play, you are simply barking up the wrong tree.

John I never thought of it, Pop.

Bradley Good. (*He crosses to sit next to John on the couch*) Did you bring up your grandfather's death?

Pause

John Yes.
Bradley I knew you would.
John I don't make a big deal of it.
Bradley I don't know why you have to make any deal of it at all.
John I think it helps say who we are.
Bradley You're always harping on it. It seems to be an obsession with you.
John I just refer to it once, Pop.
Bradley How? What do you say?
John Oh, well . . .
Bradley I want to know what you say about my father.
John I say he was a good man, a kind man, one of the best lawyers in town . . .
Bradley True enough . . .
John A leader in the community. A pillar of the church . . .
Bradley True . . . All true . . .
John Who, one day, for no discernible reason, strolled down to the edge of the Niagara River, hung his hat, his coat, and his cane on a wooden piling, and then walked into the water and drowned himself.

Pause

Bradley That's what you say in your play?
John That's what I say, Pop.

Pause

Bradley He left a note.
John I didn't know that, Pop.
Bradley Oh yes. There was a note in his breast pocket. Addressed to me and my mother. I have it in my safe deposit box.
John I didn't know he left a note.
Bradley You can have it when I die. (*Pause*) He says there will be enough money to support my mother and to send me through college. (*Pause*) Which there was. (*Pause*) Then he says he's terribly, terribly sorry, but he's come to the conclusion that life isn't worth living any more. (*Pause. He turns away from John, takes out a handkerchief and dries his eyes*)
John Oh, Pop.
Bradley Churchill had those dark moments.
John So does my son Jack.
Bradley Jack too? That sweet Jack?
John He gets it in spades.
Bradley Of course, it's just . . . life, isn't it? It's part of the equation. The point is, we don't complain, we deal with it. We divert ourselves. We play golf, we have a drink occasionally.
John We write plays.
Bradley Well, we do *some*thing. What does that sweet Jack do?
John Builds model airplanes.
Bradley Oh that poor boy. That poor, poor boy.

John Yeah, I know.

Pause

Bradley And your play gets into all this?
John A little.
Bradley Sounds like a very depressing play.
John It has its darker moments.
Bradley But no plot.
John Not really. No.
Bradley (*getting up*) Seems to me, you have to have some twist or some-
thing. I mean, it's your business, not mine, but it seems to me you need
some secret or surprise or something. I thought all plays had to have that.
John Actually, there is. A little one. At the end of the first act.
Bradley What is it?
John Oh well.
Bradley Tell it to me.
John You don't want to hear, Pop.
Bradley Tell it to me anyway.
John You'll just get angry, Pop.
Bradley I want to hear it. Please.

Pause

John All right. At the end of the first act, I have this older man ...
Bradley Me. I'm sure it's me.
John It's you and it's not you, Pop.
Bradley What does this fellow do?
John He tells his older son ...
Bradley You.
John *Partly* me, Pop. Just *partly*.
Bradley Tells his son what?
John The father tells his son that he doesn't believe ...
Bradley Doesn't believe what?
John Doesn't believe his son is his true son.
Bradley *What?*
John He says he thinks his wife once had an affair, and the son is the result.
Bradley That is the most ridiculous thing I ever heard in my life!
John I knew you'd get sore.
Bradley Of course I'm sore. Who wouldn't get sore? Where in God's name
did you get such a ridiculous idea?
John I don't know. It just happened. As I was writing.
Bradley Thank God this play is not going on! It's demeaning to me, and
insulting to your mother! Why in heaven's name would you ever want to
write a thing like that?
John Because I don't think you ever loved me, Pop.

A telephone rings off stage

Bradley That's Jigger.

The telephone rings again as Bradley hurriedly exits up the stairs, and then gives a half ring as Bradley's voice is heard answering from off-stage

Bradley (*off*) Hello? ...

John sits on the couch, looking after his father, then looking at his glass

Curtain

ACT II

Immediately after. John is sitting on the couch. His glass is now empty

Nina comes in with a plate of carrot sticks and celery

Nina Here are more munchies. It might be a little while before we eat.

John What's new with Jigger?

Nina I don't know. I just had a chance to say hello. But I know how these things work. Mother will get on the phone in their bedroom, and Pop will be on the extension in the guest room, and everyone will talk at once. (*She finds her glass*) Don't you want to get in on the act?

John I'll wait till things settle down.

Nina We're lucky that whoosie out there in the kitchen missed up on the meat. I told her we'll be a minimum of twenty minutes, during which time she can at least *think* about making gravy.

John You know. I just thought: isn't this familiar?

Nina What?

John This. You and me. Sitting here. Stomachs growling. Waiting to eat.

Nina Because of the cocktail hour ...

John Because of Jigger.

Nina It wasn't always Jigger.

John Most of the time it was. I was the good little boy, remember? I'd dash home, do my homework, wash my hands, brush my hair, sit here all during cocktails, and then just as we were about to eat, Jigger would call to say that he was still at some game or something.

Nina Sometimes.

John All the time. So you'd dig into another one of your Albert Payson Terhune dog books, and Mother and Pop would have another drink and talk about their day, and I'd just sit here stewing.

Nina That's your problem.

John Well, it was the maid's problem, too, remember? All those maids, over the years, coming to the doorway in their rustly, starchy uniforms and saying, "Dinner is served, Missus," and Mother would say, "Give us five more minutes, Mabel, or Jean, or Agnes, or whatever your name is this month," but it wouldn't be five, it would be fifteen, it would be half an *hour*, before Jigger got home and our parents would rise from the couch and stagger into the dining room to eat.

Nina They never staggered, John.

John No, you're right. They held it beautifully. The cook held dinner beautifully. And the maid kept the plates warm. The cocktail hour kept all of life in an amazing state of suspended animation.

Nina But oh those meals! Remember those *meals*? Three courses. Soup, a roast, home-made rolls, a home-made dessert! Floating Island, Brown Betty, Pineapple Upside Down Cake . . .

John Stewed prunes . . .

Nina Only occasionally. And even that was good!

John Maybe. But how did those poor souls put up with us night after night? Well, of course, they didn't. They lasted a month or two and then quit, one after the other. We were lucky that one of them didn't appear in the doorway some night with a machine gun and mow us all down!

Nina Oh, honestly, John. We were good to everyone who worked for us. We'd always go out in the kitchen and make a huge fuss.

John Oh sure, and cadge an extra cookie while the poor things were trying frantically to clean up. Oh God, Nina, what shits we were about maids!

Nina We drove them to church, we paid their medical bills . . . (*She takes her shoes off and sprawls on the couch*)

John We were shits! When Grandmother died, she left five hundred dollars to each of the three maids that had served her all her life, and the Packard to the chauffeur.

Nina Mother made it up to them.

John Oh sure. She tried. And they tried to make it up to themselves all along the way. Remember the one who stole all that liquor? Or the one who started the fire, smoking in the cedar closet? Or the one who went stark raving mad at breakfast and chased Mother around with a butter knife? Oh they had their moments of revenge. But we still built our life on their backs. Has it ever occurred to you that every dinner party, every cocktail hour, good Lord, every civilized endeavour in this world is based on exploiting the labour of the poor Cheryl Maries toiling away off stage.

Nina Her name is Shirley Marie. (*Pause*) I think. (*Pause*) And she's exploiting *us*. She's probably getting fifty bucks for three hours work, when Mother and I did most of it anyway.

John There you go. Now we're exploiting each other. Pop always carries on about the importance of civilized life, but think of what it costs to achieve it. Between what Freud tells us we do to ourselves, and what Marx tells us we do to each other, it's a wonder we don't crawl up our own assholes.

Nina Nicely put, John. All I know is, according to your good wife, Ellen, whenever you and she give a party in New York, you're the first one to want to hire some poor out-of-work actor to serve the soup.

John Yeah, I know. It's a shitty system, but I can't think of a better one.

Nina (*getting up and making another drink*) I think *you're* a shit, John. I'll say that much.

John What else is new?

Nina No, I mean now. Tonight. For this.

John For this?

Nina Coming up here. Stirring things up. With your play.

John This is probably one of the most decent things I've ever done.

Nina Badgering two old people? Threatening them with some ghastly kind of exposure in the last years of their lives?

John I came here to get their permission.

Nina You came here to stir things *up*, John. You came here to cause trouble. That's what you've done since the day you were born, and that's what you'll do till you die. You cannot let people alone, can you? A rainy day, a Sunday afternoon, every evening when you finished your homework, off you'd go on your appointed rounds, wandering from room to room in this house, teasing, causing an argument, starting a fight, leaving a trail of upset and unhappy people behind you. And when you finished with all of us, you'd go down in the kitchen and start on the cook. And when the cook left, you'd tease your teachers at school. And now that you're writing plays, you tease the critics! Anyone in authority comes under your guns. Why don't you at least be constructive about it, and tease the Mafia or the C.I.A., for God's sake? (*She sits in a chair opposite him*)

John Because I'm not a political person.

Nina Then what kind of person *are* you, John? Why are you so passionately concerned with disturbing the peace? I mean, here we are, the family at least partially together for the first time in several years, and possibly the last time in our lives, and what happens: you torment us with this play, you accuse us of running a slave market in the kitchen, you make us all feel thoroughly uncomfortable. Have you ever thought about this, John? Has it ever come to mind that this is what you do?

John Yes.

Nina Good. I'm so glad. Why do you suppose you do it?

John (*moving around the room*) Because there's a hell of a lot of horseshit around, and I think I've known it from the beginning.

Nina Would you care to cite chapter and verse?

John Sure. Horseshit begins at home.

Nina He's a wonderful man.

John He's a hypocrite, kiddo! He's a fake!

Nina Sssh!

John Talk about civilization. All that jazz about manners and class and social obligation. He's a poor boy who married a rich girl and doesn't want to be called on it.

Nina That is a lie! He was only poor after his father died!

John (*with increasing passion*) Yes, well, all that crap about hard work and nose to the grindstone and burning the midnight oil. What is all that crap? Have you ever seen it in operation? Whenever I tried to call him at the office, he was out playing golf. Have you ever *seen* him *work*? Has he ever brought any work *home*? Have you ever heard him even talk on the *telephone* about work? Have you ever seen him spade the garden or rake a leaf or change a light bulb? I remember one time when I wrote that paper defending the New Deal, he gave me a long lecture about how nobody wants to work in this country, and all the while he was practising his putting on the back lawn!

Nina He's done extremely well in business. He sent us to private schools and first-rate colleges.

John Oh, I know he's done well—on charm, affability, and Mother's money—and a little help from his friends. His friends have carried him all his life. They're the ones who have thrown the deals his way. You ask him a financial question, he'll say, "Wait a minute, I'll call Bill or Bob or Ted."

Nina Because that's *life*, John! That's what business *is*! The golf course, the backgammon table at the Mid-Day Club, the Saturn Club grille at six — that's where he *works*, you jerk!

John Well then that's where his family is, not here! Did he ever show you how to throw a ball or dive into a pool? Not him. Mother did all that, while he was off chumming it up with his pals. All he ever taught me was how to hold a fork or answer an invitation or cut in on a pretty girl. He's never been my father and I've never been his son, and he and I have known that for a long time. (*Pause. He sits exhaustedly on the piano bench*)

Nina Well, he's been a wonderful father to me.

John Maybe so. And maybe to Jigger. I guess that's why I've teased both of you all my life. And why I tease everybody else, for that matter. I'm jealous of anyone who seems to have a leg up on life, anyone who seems to have a father in the background helping them out. Hell, I even tease my own children. I've bent over backwards to be to them what my father never was to me, and then out of some deep-grained jealousy that they have it too good, I tease the pants off them.

Nina Jesus, John, you're a mess.

John I know. But I'd be more of one if I didn't write about it.

Nina Well, write as much as you want, but don't go public on this one.

John I've already said I won't.

Nina I'm not sure I believe you, John. You're too angry. You'll change a few words, a few names, and out it will come.

John Nina, I promise . . .

Nina Then how come that cheque is still there? Mother told me about the cheque, and there it is. How come?

John I don't want it.

Nina (*bringing it to him*) Take it, John. Take it, just so I'll be sure. I know you're gentleman enough not to do it if you take the dough.

John I'll never cash it. (*He takes the cheque*)

Nina I don't care, but it's yours now, and the play stays in your desk drawer now, until they're both dead. And until *I'm* dead, goddamnit.

John (*putting the cheque in his wallet*) Or until he changes his mind.

Nina Fair enough. (*She returns to the couch for more food*)

John (*putting his wallet away*) Actually I'm kind of glad it's not going on, Nina.

Nina Why?

John Because, to tell you the truth, I haven't got the plot right yet.

Nina What's wrong with it?

John I dunno. It's not right yet. It's not true yet. There's a secret in it somewhere, and I haven't quite nailed it down.

Nina What secret?

John Oh, simply the secret of what went wrong between my father and me. Where, when, why did he turn his countenance from me? There must have been a point. Did I wake him too early in the morning with my infant wails before one of those constantly replaceable nurses jammed a bottle in my mouth? Or rather *refused* to jam a bottle in my mouth because I wasn't crying on schedule?

Nina Here we go . . .

John Or when I was displayed to family and friend, did I embarrass him by playing with my pee-pee?

Nina John, you have an absolute obsession with your own penis.

John Or—*I* know! Maybe this is what I did: I made the unpardonable mistake of contradicting him—of looking something *up* in the Book of Knowledge, and proving him wrong—no, not wrong, that makes no difference, right or wrong—what I did was destroy the "rhythm of the conversation," maybe that's what I did wrong!

Nina Oh good Lord . . .

John Yes well, I'd love to know what I did to have him say to himself—and to *me*!—"I don't know this boy. This is not my son." Because he's said it as long as I can remember.

Nina And if he ever told you he loved you, you'd immediately do some totally irritating thing to make him deny it.

John You think so?

Nina I know so. If he killed the fatted calf, you'd complain about the cholesterol.

John Jesus, Nina.

Nina You would. I've got your number, John, even if you don't have mine. For instance, I know why you're writing this goddamn play.

John Why?

Nina (*hurriedly, as she puts on her shoes*) You're writing it because he's dying. You're writing it because you love him. You're writing it to hold onto him after he's gone.

Ann enters

Ann John, don't you want to speak to your brother before your father hangs up.

John Sure.

John angrily grabs some carrots and exits upstairs

Ann (*distractedly*) Well, that's that.

Nina What?

Ann (*vaguely*) I'd like a splash more, please, Nina.

Nina (*getting Ann's glass and going to the bar*) All right.

Ann Just a splash. I'm serious.

Nina All right.

Ann (*sinking onto the couch*) I give up.

Nina What's the *trouble*, Mother?

Ann Jigger. Jigger's the trouble. He wants to move to California.

Nina What?

Ann He wants to pick up stakes and move. Wife, children, off they go.

Nina What's in California?

Ann A job. A new job. There's a man out there who builds wooden boats, who wants Jigger to work for him. For *half* of what he's making now.

Nina But why?

Ann Because he wants to. He says it's something he's always wanted to do.

Nina He's always liked boats.

Ann Don't I know it. That canoe he built in the basement. Those sailboats out on the lake . . .

Nina (*joining her on the couch*) Which had to be *wood*, remember? No fibreglass allowed. All that labour every spring, because only wood sat naturally on the water . . .

Ann Between his boats and your dogs we hardly had time to think around here.

Nina He felt free on the water. I wish *I* felt free about something.

Ann Well I hear they feel free about *every*thing in California.

Nina And he's just . . . going?

Ann Says he is. Says he plans to buy one of those grubby vans, and lug everyone out, like a bunch of Oakies. Your father is frantically trying to talk him out of it.

Nina (*musingly*) I should just go to Cleveland to that dog school.

Ann Oh, Nina. Think of Ed.

Nina I *have* thought of Ed. We've talked about it. He says, do it. Which makes it all the harder.

Ann I should hope so.

Nina Still. Maybe I should. I should just do it. What would you say if I did it, Mother?

Ann Go to *Cleve*land?

Nina Three days a week.

Ann Just to be with *dogs*?

Nina To *work* with them, Mother.

Ann I've never understood your fascination with dogs.

Nina I don't know. When I'm with them, I feel I'm in touch with something . . . basic.

Ann Horses I can understand. The thrill of riding. The excitement of the hunt. The men.

Nina The men?

Ann There used to be a lot of attractive men around stables.

Nina Mother!

Ann Just as there are around garages today.

Nina Are you serious?

Ann But I don't think they hang around kennels.

Nina I'm interested in *dogs*, Mother.

Ann I know you are, darling, and I don't think that's any reason to change your life. I mean if you had met some man . . .

Nina Mother, have you ever watched any of those Nature things on TV?

Ann I love them. Every Sunday night . . .

Nina I mean, you see animals, birds, even insects operating under these incredibly complicated instincts. Courting, building their nests, rearing their young in the most amazing complex way . . .

Ann Amazing behaviour . . .

Nina Well, I think people have these instincts, too.

Ann Well, I'm sure we do darling, but——

Nina No, but I mean many more than we realize. I think they're built into our blood, and I think we're most alive when we feel them happening to us.

Ann Oh well now, I don't know . . .

Nina I feel most alive when I'm with animals, Mother. Really. I feel some instinctive connection. Put me with a dog, a cat, anything, and I feel I'm in touch with a whole different dimension . . . It's as if both of us . . . me and the animal . . . were reaching back across hundreds of thousands of years to a place where we both knew each other much better. There's something there, Mother. I know there's something there.

Ann Oh Nina, you sound like one of those peculiar women who wander around Africa falling in love with gorillas.

Nina Maybe I do. (*Pause*) I hope I do. (*Pause*) I'd rather sound like that than just an echo of you, Mother.

Ann Well. I think we're all getting too wound up over boats and dogs. People, yes. Boats and dogs, no. The whole family seems to be suddenly going to pieces over boats and dogs.

Nina And plays, Mother.

Ann Yes. All right. And plays.

Bradley enters from upstairs

Bradley We've lost him.

Ann Oh now, darling.

Bradley We've lost him.

Ann Oh no.

Bradley I'll never see him again.

Ann Oh, darling.

Bradley I'll be lucky if he comes to my funeral.

Ann Now, now. I'll tell you one thing. A good *meal* will make us all feel much better.

Nina I'll tell Shirley.

Bradley Her name is Sharon.

Ann I still think it's Cheryl.

Nina Well, whatever it is, I'll tell her we're ready to *eat*!

Nina exits

Bradley goes to the bar

Ann I wouldn't drink any more, sweetie. We're about to eat.

Bradley I need this.

Ann How about some wine with dinner? We'll have that.

Bradley Wine won't do it.

Ann Oh, Bradley . . .

Bradley (*moving around the room*) I've lost my son. My son is moving three thousand miles away. I'm too old and sick and tired to go see him. And he'll be too tied up in his work to come see me.

Ann (*following him*) Oh now, sweetheart . . .

Bradley There are men, there are men in this world whose sons stay with them all the days of their lives. Fred Tillinghast's sons *work* with him every day at the office. He has lunch with them at noon, he has cocktails with them at night, he plays golf with them on weekends. They discuss everything together. Money, women, they're always completely at ease. When he went to Europe, those boys went with him and carried his bags. What did he do to deserve such luck? What did he do that I didn't? I've given my sons everything. I gave them an allowance every week of their lives. I gave them stock. I gave them the maximum deductible gift every Christmas. And now what happens? I reach my final years, my final moments, the nadir of my life, and one son attacks me while the other deserts me. Oh, it is not to be borne, my love. It is not to be borne. (*He sinks into his chair*)

Ann Oh, now just wait, Bradley. Maybe John is talking him out of it.

Bradley John?

Ann John always had a big influence on him.

Bradley John? Jigger and John have fought all their lives. *I'm* the influence. I'm the father. What can John possibly say that I haven't said?

John enters quickly

John I told him he should go.

Bradley You didn't.

Ann John!

John Sure. I said, go on. Make your move!! How many guys in the world get a chance to do what they really want?

Bradley I should never have let you near the telephone.

Ann I'm not sure that was entirely helpful, John.

Bradley He has a fine job where he is.

John Pushing papers around a desk. Dealing with clients all weekend.

Bradley That's an excellent job. He has a decent salary. He's made all sorts of friends. I got him that job through Phil Foster.

John You might as well know something else, Pop. I got him this new one.

Bradley You?

John I put him on to it. The boatyard is owned by a college classmate of mine. I read about it in the *Alumni Review* and got an interview for Jigger.

Bradley Why?

John Because he was miserable where he was.

Bradley I should have known you were behind all this . . .

John He hated that job, Pop. Now he can work with boats, and join the Sierra Club, and do all that stuff he loves to do.

Bradley It was none of your damn business.

John He's my brother!

Bradley I'm his father! Me!

Nina enters

John Well, I'm glad he's going, Pop. And I think Nina should work in Cleveland, too . . . I think you should, Nina.

Nina I think I will.

Ann Oh Nina, no!

Bradley That's ridiculous.

John So what if Ed has to cook his own spaghetti occasionally . . .

Nina He'd do it gladly.

Bradley Nonsense. Ed can't cook spaghetti . . .

Nina No. I think I'll do it. I think I'll go. I'll stay there, and study there, and come home when I can. Put that in your play and write it, John.

John Maybe I will.

Nina Sure. Have the goddess Diana come downstage and plant her feet, and give this marvellous speech about seeing-eye dogs, which will bring the audience rising to its feet, and cause your friends the critics to systematically pee in their pants!

Ann That's not attractive, Nina.

John I don't know. I kind of liked it.

Bradley You kind of like playing God around here, don't you?

Ann Yes, John, I really think you should stop managing other people's lives.

Bradley Yes. Do that in your plays if you have to, not in real life.

John Oh yeah? Well, I'm glad we're talking about real life now, Pop. Because that's something we could use a little more *of*, around here. Hey. Know what? The cocktail hour is over, Pop. It's dead. It's gone. I think Jigger sensed it thirty years ago, and now Nina knows it too, and they're both *trying* to put something back into the world after all these years of a free ride.

Bradley And you? What are you putting back into the world?

John Me?

Bradley You.

John I'm writing about it. At least I have the balls to do that.

Bradley Leave this room!

Ann Oh Bradley . . .

John Maybe I should leave altogether.

Bradley Maybe you should.

Nina Oh Pop . . .

John (*grabbing his bag in the hall*) Lucky I didn't unpack . . .

Ann John, now stop . . .

John (*throwing on his raincoat*) Call Ellen, Nina. Tell her I'm coming home. Say I'm banished because of my balls!

Bradley I will not allow you to speak vulgarities in this house.

John Balls? Balls are vulgar?

Ann Now that's enough.

John (*coming back into the room*) Does that mean you don't have any, Pop? Does that mean we should all just sit on our ass and watch the world go by?

Ann (*going to the front hall*) I think it's time to eat.

Bradley I'll tell you what it means. It means that vulgar people always fall back on vulgar language.

Ann (*beckoning to Nina*) What's the food situation, Nina?

Bradley It means that there are more important things in the world than bodily references.

Ann (*at the doorway*) Food! Yoo-hoo, everybody! Food!

Bradley It means that your mother and I, and your grandparents on both sides, and Aunt Jane and Uncle Roger and Cousin Esther, and your forbears who came to this country in the seventeenth *century* have all spent their lives trying to establish something called civilization in this wilderness, and as long as I am alive, I will not allow foul-minded and resentful people to tear it all down.

He storms off and upstairs. There is a long pause

Ann Well. You were right about one thing, John: the cocktail hour is definitely over.

Nina Um. Not quite, Mother.

Ann What do you mean?

Nina Come sit down, Mother.

Ann Don't tell me there is more bad news from the kitchen.

Nina (*going to her*) The roast beef is a little the worse for wear.

Ann What?

Nina The roast is ruined.

Ann No.

Nina Sheila got confused.

Ann Sheila?

Nina It's *Sheila* Marie. I know, because I just made out her cheque and said she could go.

Ann What did she do?

Nina She thought that microwave thing was a warming oven. It came out looking like a shrunken head.

Ann Oh, I can't *stand* it!

Nina The peas are still good, and I found some perfectly adequate lamb chops in the freezer. They won't take too long.

Ann Thank you, darling. Would you tell your father? I imagine he's upstairs in the television room, cooling off on the hockey game.

Nina (*taking one of the hors d'oeuvres plates*) I'll take him up some cheese, just to hold him.

Nina exits and goes upstairs

Ann (*calling after her*) You're a peach, Nina. You really are. Those dogs don't deserve you. (*Pause*) That was an absolutely lovely rib roast of beef.

John I'm sure.

Ann Twenty-eight dollars. At the Ex-Cell.

John I can believe it.

Ann I suppose Portia might like it. Nina can give it to Portia.

John Good idea.

Pause

Ann (*beginning to clean up*) I don't know why I'm talking to you, John. I'm
very angry. You've caused nothing but trouble since the minute you
arrived.

John Story of my life.

Ann I'm afraid it is.

John I wish I knew why.

Ann Isn't that what your psychiatrist is supposed to explain, at one hundred
dollars a throw?

John He never could.

Ann Then I was right: They're a waste of money. (*She starts to go out*) I'd
better check on those lamb chops.

John Mother . . .

She stops

Since I've been here, I've discovered a big problem with this play of mine.

Ann I'd say it had lots of problems. In my humble opinion.

John Well I've discovered a big one. It's missing an obligatory scene.

Ann And what in heaven's name is that?

John It's a scene which sooner or later has to happen. It's an essential scene.
Without it, everyone walks out feeling discontent and frustrated.

Ann I suppose you mean some ghastly confrontation with your father.

John Hell no. I've got plenty of those.

Ann You've got too many of those.

John I'm thinking of a scene with you, Mother.

Ann With me?

John That's what's been missing all my life, Mother.

Ann Oh, John, please don't get melodramatic. (*She starts to go out again*)

John I've also discovered why it's been missing.

Ann Why?

John Because you don't want it to happen.

Ann I'll tell you what I want to have happen, John. I want us all to sit down
together and have a pleasant meal. That's all I want to have happen at the
moment, thank you very much.

John (*leading her to the couch*) Oh come on, Mother. Please. This is the ideal
moment. Pop's sulking upstairs. Nina's busy in the kitchen. And you and
I are both a little smashed, which will make it easier. Tell me just one
thing.

Ann What thing?

John What went wrong when I was very young. Something went wrong.
There was some short circuit . . . some problem . . . something . . . What
was it?

Ann I don't know what you're talking about.

John Come on, Mother. Please. Think back.

Ann (*getting up*) John, I am not going to sit around and rake over a lot of
old coals. Life's too short and I'm too old, and thank you very much.

She goes out to the kitchen

John (*calling after her*) And once again, there goes the obligatory scene, right out the door!

A moment, then Ann comes back in, putting on an apron

Ann You got lost in the shuffle, John. That's what went wrong. I mean, there you were, born in the heart of the Depression, your father frantic about money, nurses and maids leaving every other day—nobody paid much attention to you, I'm afraid. When Nina was born, we were all dancing around thinking we were the Great Gatsby, and when Jigger came along, we began to settle down. But you, poor soul, were caught in the middle. You lay in your crib screaming for attention, and I'm afraid you've been doing it ever since.

John That's it?

Ann That's it. In a nutshell. Now I feel very badly about it, John. I always have. That's why I've found it hard to talk about. I've worked hard to make it up, I promise, but sometimes, no matter how hard you work, you just can't hammer out all the dents. (*She turns to leave again*)

John Exit my mother, after a brief, unsatisfactory exchange ...

Ann That's right. Because your mother is now responsible for a meal.

John (*blocking her way*) I can see the scene going on just a tad longer, Mother.

Ann How?

John I think there's more to be said.

Ann About what?

John About you, Mother.

Ann Me?

John You. I think there's much more to be said about you.

Ann Such as?

John Such as, where were you, while the king was in the counting house and the kid was in his cradle?

Ann I was ... here, of course.

John Didn't you pick me up, if I was screaming in my crib?

Ann Yes. Sometimes. Yes.

John But not enough?

Ann No. Not enough.

John Why not?

Pause

Ann Because ... because at that point I was a little preoccupied.

John With what?

Ann Oh, John.

John With what?

Ann I don't have to say.

John With *what*, Mother?

Pause

Ann I was writing a book.

John You were what?

Ann I was sitting right at that desk, all day, every day, writing a big, long book. It took too much of my time, and too much of my thoughts, and I'm sorry if it made me neglect you ... I've never told anyone about that book.

John Doesn't it feel good to tell me?

Ann Not particularly. No. (*She sits at the desk*)

John What happened to it?

Ann I burned it.

John You burned it?

Ann All six hundred and twenty-two pages of it. Right in that fireplace. One day, while your father was playing golf.

John Why?

Ann Because I didn't like it. I couldn't get it right. It was wrong.

John Wow, Mother!

Ann I know it. (*Pause*) But then we had Jigger, and that took my mind off it.

John What was the book about, Mother?

Ann I won't tell.

John Oh, come on.

Ann I've never told a soul.

John One writer to another, Mother.

Ann Never.

John You mean, the book you wrote instead of nursing me, the book that took my place at your breast ...

Ann Oh, John, really.

John The six-hundred page book that preoccupied your mind during a crucial formative period of my own, I'll never get to know about. Boy. Talk about hammering our dents, Mother. You've just bashed in my entire front end.

Pause

Ann I'll give you a brief summary of the plot.

John OK.

Ann Brief. You'll have to fill things in as best you can.

John OK. (*He quickly gets a chair from the hall, and straddles it, next to her*)

Ann (*taken aback*) First, though, I will have a splash more.

John Sure.

Ann Just a splash. I'm serious.

John All right, Mother. (*He hurriedly mixes her martini*)

Ann I mean, it's no easy thing to tell one's own son one's innermost thoughts. Particularly when that son tends to be slightly critical.

John I won't criticize, Mother. I swear. (*He brings her her drink and again straddles the chair beside her*)

Ann (*after taking a sip*) All right, then. My book was about a woman.

John A woman.

Ann A governess.

John A governess?

Ann A well-born woman who goes to work for a distinguished man and supervises the upbringing of his children.

John Sounds like *Jane Eyre*.
Ann If you make any cracks, I won't tell you any more.
John Sorry, Mother. It sounds good.
Ann Now, this woman, this governess, does *not* fall in love with her employer. Unlike Jane Eyre.
John She does not?
Ann No. She falls in love with someone else.
John Someone else.
Ann She falls in love with a groom.
John A groom?
Ann A very attractive groom. At the stable. Where she keeps her horse.
John I'm with you, Mother.
Ann She has a brief, tempestuous affair with the man who saddles her horse.
John I see.
Ann Well, it doesn't work out, so she terminates the affair. But the groom gets so upset, he sets fire to the stable.
John Sets fire.
Ann The fire symbolizes his tempestuous passion.
John I see.
Ann Naturally, she rushes into the flames to save the horses. And she gets thoroughly burned. All over her face. It's horrible.
John She is punished, in other words, for her indiscretion.
Ann Yes. That's right. That's it exactly. But finally her wounds heal. The doctor arrives to take off the bandages. Everyone stands around to see. And guess what? She is perfectly beautiful. She is even more beautiful than she was before. The children cluster around her, the master of the house embraces her, and so she marries this man who has loved her all along. You see? Her experience has helped her. In the long run. (*Pause*) Anyway, that's the end. (*Pause*) You can see why I burned it. (*Pause*) You can see why I haven't told anyone about it, all these years. (*Pause*) It's terribly corny, isn't it?
John No, Mother.
Ann It's silly.
John No, it says a lot. (*He kisses her on the cheek*)
Ann John, you're embarrassing me.
John No, really. It's very touching.
Ann Well, I never could get the *feelings* right. Especially with that groom. That passion. The tempestuous passion. Those . . . flames. I could never get that right in my book.
John I never could either, in a play.
Ann Oh, it would be impossible in a play.
John Maybe.
Ann That's why I wish you would write a good, long, wonderful book. (*She gets up*) And now I really ought to give Nina a hand with supper.
John Mother, one more question . . .
Ann You've asked too many.
John About the groom.
Ann Ah, the groom.

John What happened to him?

Ann Oh heavens. I can't remember. I think I sent him off to Venezuela or somewhere.

John In the book?

Ann In the book.

Ann But what happened in life, Mother?

Ann In *life*?

John Where did he go? Who was he?

Ann I never said he *existed*, John. This ... groom.

John But he did, didn't he? You met him before you had me. And he left after I was born. And you sat down and wrote about him. Now come on. Who was he?

Ann John ...

John Please, Mother. Tell me.

Ann It was over forty years ago ...

John Still, Mother. Come on. Whom did you base him on?

Ann Oh, John, I don't know ... Maybe I'm getting old ... or maybe I've had too many cocktails ... but I'm beginning to think I based him on your father.

She starts to go out as Bradley enters

Bradley Based what on me?

Ann My life, darling. I've based my life on you.

She kisses him and exits. Pause

Bradley Your mother always knows when to walk out of a room.

John My mother is full of surprises.

Bradley Well, she instinctively senses when a man needs to do business with another man. And out she goes.

John We're going to do business, Pop?

Bradley (*going to his chair*) We're going to talk seriously. And I hope when you have to talk seriously with one of your sons, your sweet Ellen will bow out just as gracefully.

John What's on your mind, Pop?

Bradley First, I'd like a glass of soda water, please.

John I'll have one, too.

Bradley Good. Time for sermons and soda water, eh?

John It sure does feel like the day after. (*He fixes the two drinks*)

Bradley John: you and I spoke angry words to each other a while back. It was most unfortunate. I blame you, I blame myself, and I blame alcohol. There's nothing more dangerous than a lengthy cocktail hour.

John I apologize, Pop. I got carried away.

Bradley We both got carried away. We screamed and shouted, didn't we? Well, at least we didn't take off our clothes.

John Here's your soda water, Pop.

Bradley Thank you, John. You know what I did upstairs instead of watching the hockey?

John What?

Bradley I sat and thought. I thought about all of you. I thought about . . . my father. Do you suppose all families are doomed to disperse?

John Most of them do, Pop. Eventually. In this country.

Bradley You don't think it's . . . me?

John No, Pop.

Bradley People seem to want to leave me. There seems to be this centrifugal force.

John That's life, Pop.

Bradley Well, whatever it is, I can't fight it any more . . . When I was upstairs, I telephoned Jigger. I called him back.

John Oh yes?

Bradley What is it Horace Greeley tells us? "Go west, young man"? Well, he's young. It's there. I gave him my blessing.

John (*sitting near him*) That's good, Pop.

Bradley "The old oak must bend with the wind . . . or break . . ." (*He looks at John*) Isn't that from Virgil?

John I think it's T. S. Eliot.

They both laugh

But don't look it up.

They laugh again

Bradley Maybe I've loved him too much. Maybe I've loved him at your expense. Do you think that's true?

Pause

John (*carefully*) I don't know . . .

Bradley Maybe he's trying to get away from me. What do you think?

John I think . . . (*Pause*) I think maybe he's trying to get away from all of us. I think maybe I got him to go because I was jealous. Hell, I think we all put our own spin on the ball—you, me, Nina, Mother—and guess what: it no longer matters. Jigger likes *boats*, Pop. He likes working with *wood*. Maybe he'll build a new clipper ship.

Bradley Well, the point is, he'll be happy there. Sailing. He's a magnificent sailor. Remember right here on Lake Erie?

John I remember . . .

Bradley I could sit in my office and look out on the lake, and sometimes I think I could actually see his sails . . .

John Yes . . .

Bradley Of course, that friend of yours is hardly paying him a nickel out there. Hardly a plug nickel. And they'll have to buy a house. I mean, they all can't live in that stupid van. Even after he sells his house here, he'll need a considerable amount of additional cash. So I told him I'd send him a cheque. (*He begins to look at, around, and under the table next to him for the cheque he gave to John*) And I told him the cupboard was a little bare, at the moment. A little bare. I'm no longer collecting a salary, as you know, and I do need to keep a little cash on hand these days. Doctors . . . Pills . . . If I should have to go into the hospital . . .

John takes the cheque out of his wallet and hands it to Bradley

John Here you go, Pop.

Bradley (*taking it*) Thank you, John. (*Pause*) I mean, I refuse to sell stock. I can't do that. When I die, I want your mother to have . . . I want all of you to have . . . I've got to leave something.

John I know, Pop.

Nina enters

Nina I think we're almost ready to eat. Just so you'll know. (*She takes the hors d'oeuvre plate and starts to go out*)

John We're discussing the National Debt.

Nina Oh. (*Then she stops*) Come to think of it, Pop, you could do me one hell of a big favour.

Bradley What, Pookins?

Nina (*going to him*) I wonder if I might ask for a little money.

Bradley Money?

Nina (*sitting on the arm of his chair*) For Cleveland. Tuition. Travel. Living expenses. It costs money to change your life.

Bradley I'm sure that Ed . . .

Nina Ed would subsidize my commuting to the moon, if I asked him. Which is why I won't. I want to get back on the gravy train for a while, Pop. I'll borrow from you and pay you back, once I have a job. It's as simple as that.

Bradley We'll work out something, Pookins. I promise.

Nina Oh thanks, Pop. I knew you would. (*She kisses him, and starts to exit gloatingly*) And as for you, John, I think you should get yourself a good dog. I'll tell you why but first I have to toss the salad.

Nina exits

Bradley I suppose she'll want at least twenty as well.

John She might.

Bradley And she should get it. It's only fair.

John Right.

Bradley I am *not* going to cut into capital.

John I know . . .

Bradley My father used to tell me every moment of his life . . .

John I know . . .

Bradley Even as it is, I'm cutting close to the bone . . .

John You'll live, Pop.

Bradley No, I won't. I'll die. But I'll die fair. I'll add twenty extra for you in my will. That's a promise. I'll call Bill Sawyer first thing.

John Thanks, Pop.

Bradley So. You all get exactly the same amount of money.

John That's right.

Bradley Jigger gets his boats . . . Nina gets her dogs . . .

John Right, Pop . . .

Bradley And all I have to worry about is that damn play.

John It's not going on, Pop.

Bradley (*getting up*) If only you'd put in some of the good things. The singing around the piano, for example. That was good. Or the skiing. That was very good. That's when we were at our best.

John It's hard to put skiing on the stage, Pop.

Bradley You could talk about it. You could at least mention it.

John I do, actually. I bring it up.

Bradley You do? You mention the skiing?

John The skiing and the piano both.

Bradley Do you think you could mention anything else?

Ann's voice is heard from off stage

Ann (*off*) I'm about to light the candles!

Bradley (*calling off*) Two more minutes, darling! Just two! (*To John*) I mean, if I were writing the darned thing, I'd want to prove to those critics we *are* worth writing about. I'd put our best foot forward, up and down the line.

John I have to call 'em as I see 'em, Pop.

Bradley That's what I'm afraid of.

Ann appears at the door

Ann Now Nina has just whipped together a perfectly spectacular meal. There's even mint sauce to go with the lamb chops. Now come on, or it will all get cold.

Bradley Just a minute more, my love. We're discussing the future of American drama.

Ann Couldn't you discuss it in the dining room?

Bradley I'm not sure I can.

Ann Well hurry, or Nina and I will sit down and dig in all by ourselves.

She exits

John takes a tie out of his jacket pocket, and begins to put it on, looking in a wall mirror

Bradley What happens at the end of this play? Do you have me die?

John No, Pop.

Bradley Sure you don't kill me off?

John Promise.

Bradley Then how do you leave me in the end?

John I'm not sure now.

Bradley You could mention my charities, for example, you could say I've tried to be very generous.

John I could ...

Bradley Or you could refer to my feelings for your mother. You should say I've adored her for almost fifty years.

John I'll think about it, Pop ...

Nina enters

Nina Those lamb chops are just lying there, looking at us!

Nina exits

Ann's laughter is heard off stage

Bradley I suppose what you need is a kicker at the end of your play.

John A kicker?

Bradley When I give a speech, I try to end with a kicker.

John A kicker.

Bradley Some final point which pulls everything together.

John In the theatre, they call that a button.

Bradley Well, whatever it is, it makes people applaud.

John You can't *make* people applaud, Pop ...

Bradley You can generate an appreciative mood. I mean, isn't that what we want, really? Both of us? In the end? Isn't that why I make speeches and you write plays? Isn't that why people go to the theatre? Don't we all want to celebrate something at the end of the day?

John I guess we do.

Bradley Of course we do. In spite of all our difficulties, surely we can agree on that. So find a good kicker for the end.

John Kicker, kicker, who's got the kicker?

Bradley (*picking up the script gingerly, like a dead fish, and handing it to him*) Meanwhile, here. Put this away somewhere, so it doesn't dominate the rest of our lives.

John (*taking it*) OK, Pop.

Bradley (*turning off various lights*) Because there are other things in the world besides plays ...

John Pop ...

Bradley Good food ... Congenial conversation ... The company of lovely women ...

John I've just thought of a kicker, Pop.

Bradley Now *please* don't settle for some smart remark.

John Pop, listen. Remember the plot I was telling you about? Where the older son thinks he's illegitimate?

Bradley (*starting to go out*) I can't discuss it.

John No, no, Pop. Wait. Please. Here's the thing: suppose in the end, he discovers he's the true son of his father, after all.

Bradley stops, turns and looks at him

Bradley That just might do it.

Ann comes in again

Ann Now come *on.* Nothing can be more important than a good meal. Bring the tray, please, John, so that we don't have to stare at a lot of old liquor bottles after dinner. (*To Bradley, taking his arm*) Wait till you see what Nina has produced for dessert ...

Bradley (*as he goes, over his shoulder, to John*) ... I still don't like your title, John. Why don't you simply call it *The Good Father?* ...

John stands, holding his play, watching his parents exit as the Lights fade quickly

CURTAIN

FURNITURE AND PROPERTY LIST

ACT I

On stage: Antique writing desk. *In it:* cheque book, pen
Working fireplace with mantelpiece
Fire bench
Impressionist painting
Hardback and leatherbound books, including "Life's Pictured History of World War II"
Baby grand piano with bench
Assorted black and white family photographs in silver and leather frames
Large comfortable couch
Coffee table. *On it:* china ashtrays, thick manuscript with a black cover
Comfortable chairs
Moveable footstool
Corner china cabinet. *In it:* china
Wall mirror
Persian rug
Table
Cocktail napkins
Needlework
Barometer
Chairs
John's raincoat and bag

Off stage: Silver ice-bucket **(Bradley)**
Silver tray. *On it:* liquor bottles, including a bottle of Cutty Sark scotch, and glasses **(John)**
Plate of cheese and crackers **(Ann)**

Personal: **John:** lemon
Bradley: handkerchief

ACT II

On stage: As before

Off stage: Plate of carrot sticks and celery **(Nina)**
Apron **(Ann)**

Personal: **John:** wallet, tie

LIGHTING PLOT

Property fittings required: wall lights

Interior. The same throughout

ACT I

To open: Light from windows indicates early evening

Cue 1	**Bradley** turns on the light in the hall	(Page 1)
	Bring up lights	

ACT II

To open: As before

Cue 2	**Bradley** turns off various lights	(Page 48)
	Snap off lights	
Cue 3	**John** stands, holding his play, watching his parents	(Page 48)
	Lights fade quickly	

EFFECTS PLOT

ACT I

Cue 1   **John:** "Because I don't think you ever loved me, Pop"   (Page 28)
           Off-stage telephone rings and then gives a half ring

ACT II

No cues

MADE AND PRINTED IN GREAT BRITAIN BY
LATIMER TREND & COMPANY LTD PLYMOUTH
MADE IN ENGLAND